This book is presented to:

Granna

With love from:

Max, REX, JAXON, Brox, Pex

Date:

Mother's Day 2013

An Everyday Grandma!

June Gordon

A Meridian Publication
Grand Rapids, Michigan

Manufactured in the United States of America

Requests for information should be addressed to:
Meridian Publications
3040 Charlevoix Drive, SE
Grand Rapids, Michigan 49546
meridian@omco.com

Managing Editor: Rebecca Humm
Project Editor: Sarah M. Hupp
Graphic Design: Joel A. Jetzer

Manufactured in the United States of America

The Faith of a Child

The huge crowd on the hillside
was hungry,
And a lad gave his fishes and bread—
Then Jesus blessed
the small loaves and two fishes,
And all of the people were fed.

Now through the ages the world
grows darker,
And each day men's deeds are more vile—
But the pathway to heaven's still open,
And it's lit by the faith of a child.

Introduction

My granddaughters are growing up. At the present time my younger granddaughter, Kara, says she wants to become a doctor. Because she experienced several trips to the emergency room at an early age, she says she remembers "how hurt feels." While she is a very serious and good student for one so young, Kara still likes to play ball with her older sister, Kristin.

Kristin is an honor student who loves to read. She still loves to play ball, too, of any kind. Though Kristin is uncertain of what she wishes to do for her life's vocation, as her grandma I'm sure that she will be playing some kind of ball in her spare time.

Though both girls are progressing through school now, when I wrote these stories Kristin was just beginning her journey through education and Kara was in preschool. Because Kristin was away at school all day, I spent a lot of time with Kara all by herself. As a result I am afraid a good share of these stories only concern Kara. I didn't mean to play favorites—life just happened that way! As I share these snippets of our lives with you, it's my wish that you will enjoy these little tales as much as I enjoyed writing them.

June Gordon

Table of Contents

We Bettah Pway

My strength is made perfect in weakness.
2 Corinthians 12:9

Kristin sat in her car seat, a happy two-year-old on the way to her favorite park. Since I am literally directionless and was not familiar with the town, Kristin's father had drawn me a detailed map of the route to the park. We arrived safely, and she spent hours in happy play. As the afternoon shadows lengthened, I knew I must take her home.

Somehow, as we left the park, I missed the right exit. Soon I had no idea where we were. I turned the car around and tried to retrace the route I had just come, hoping that I could return to the park and begin again in the right direction towards home.

Consternation registered in Kristin's blue eyes. Even at the tender age of two, Kristin was aware of Grandma's failing. She knew we were lost and she exclaimed soberly,"Gwandma! We bettah pway!"

I smiled and said, "We will pray. And I know God will help us find our way home."

I did manage to return to the park, find the correct exit, and find our way back to Kristin's home.

And as I unloaded my granddaughter I realized that in Grandma's weakness Kristin had seen God's power. While I have often felt embarrassed because I have no inner radar for directions, this time I felt humbled. God had let my shortcomings point my granddaughter to His power and loving care.

Dear Lord, thank you that as a toddler Kristin learned to turn to you for help. Remind me to follow her childlike example when I face problems too.

My Daddy Knows My Name!

Before I formed you in the womb I knew you.
Jeremiah 1:5

When my granddaughter Kristin was three years old, I took her for a ride in her little red wagon. I decided it would be a good opportunity to teach her how to identify herself in the unlikely event that she might sometime get lost. I told her that if she should ever become separated from her family or friends, she should find a policeman and tell him that her name was Kristin Elizabeth Niemeir and that her address was 1306 East 19th, Newton, Kansas.*

Kristin parroted the information quickly: "Kiston Ewesebef Nemire, Firteen-o-six Est Nineteenth, Nuton, Tansas."* I smiled at her, and we continued the ride.

Returning home, as I parked her little wagon and she dismounted, I told her to go tell her daddy what her name and address were. She approached her father who was working in the yard, and, having obtained his attention told him: "Firteen-o-six Est Nineteenth, Nuton, Tansas."*

I smiled and said, "Honey that's right, but tell Daddy your name first."

Kristin shrugged her shoulders and lifted her hands in an expression of utter disdain as she replied, "Gwandma! My daddy knows my name!"

I thought, *How true!* And how wonderfully true, too, that we have a heavenly Father who knows our names— each one of us individually. God told the prophet Jeremiah that he knew him before Jeremiah was ever formed in his mother's womb and that he had ordained Jeremiah to be a prophet.

I believe that God knows each one of us, too, before we are formed and that he has special tasks for each of us to do—tasks peculiarly fitted to our God-given abilities. Aren't you glad God knows your name?

Dear heavenly Father, thank you for your great love that knows all of your children and their abilities from before the time they are born. Please help each one of us to do the work you have given us.

* Fictional Address

A Good Name

A good name is to be chosen rather than great riches.
Proverbs 22:1

Kristin has a little sister who is four years younger than she is. Her name is Kara Rebekah. We had shortened her name to KaraBeck, KaraBecky, or just Becky. But one day early in her life, my younger granddaughter decided she didn't like these nicknames. She wanted to be called by her right name—either Kara or Kara Rebekah. Though it was hard to remember not to use the nicknames, because we loved her we tried to honor her wishes. It was so important to Kara.

A person's name is important. We may have known families who have such an honorable reputation we feel that we can trust anyone who carries the family name. Sometimes, too, special family names are given to children in remembrance of an ancestor or special event.

The Bible also regards a person's name as highly important. Names were changed at times in order to describe a change in the person. Abram became Abraham—meaning, "father of nations." Jesus told Simon that his name would be Peter—meaning, "Rock"—and Saul's name was changed to Paul.

Often these name changes occurred when the individuals involved made a deep commitment to faith in God. When we make a commitment to faith in Christ as our Savior, we are given a new name too—the name Christian, a name first given to Jesus' followers at Antioch. As Christians we are part of the family of God.

Dear heavenly Father, please help me through the power of your Holy Spirit to only bring honor to the beauty and glory of your name. May I always follow Christ's teachings so that people will recognize and honor you and the good name I have been given as your child.

Somebody Cares

A new commandment I give to you, that you love one another; as I have loved you. ...By this all will know that you are My disciples, if you have love for one another.

John 13:34-35

"**Y**ou don't care 'bout me!" Kara cried angrily. Tears rolled down her face. She felt neglected and left out. But that was never my intention.

During a visit to my daughter's home, I had prepared a bountiful breakfast for the family. When I saw that my granddaughter Kara was sleeping soundly, I did not awaken her to join us for breakfast. Our voices, however, aroused her. Believe me, it took some explanations and apologies to soothe her hurt feelings.

There are times when all of us feel left out—times when we feel no one cares about us. But there is somebody who always cares: Jesus. An old song my Aunt Lottie used to sing entitled "Somebody Cares" contained the words:

Somebody cares when you're lonely,
Tired, discouraged and blue;
Somebody wants you to know Him,
And know He dearly loves you.
His name? We call His name Jesus;
He loves everyone, He loves you.[1]

There is a deep need within each one of us to feel loved. Jesus understands that need. At the Last Supper, Jesus commanded his disciples to love each other, even as he had loved them. Since Jesus always loves and cares for each and every one of us in spite of our failures and shortcomings, that's a big order! A song we sing at church declares, "they'll know we are Christians by our love."[2] When we can love each other as Jesus loves us, people will recognize that we are Christians and see that we care about others because Jesus cares about us all.

Dear Lord, thank you for your love. Help me to pass it on to others and show them that you do care about them.

Jesus Pwayed for Me!

It is Christ who died, and furthermore is also risen, who is even at the right hand of God, who also makes intercession for us.
Romans 8:34

It was a beautiful late summer Sunday, and I watched Kara, then three years old, swing higher and higher on the swing set, the pure abandonment of joyful play wreathing her face. My niece Barb mentioned that there was a hint of fall in the air, when suddenly there was a shriek of pain. Kara was crying and screaming.

I ran to her. As I gathered her in my arms, Kara's blood soaked my clothing, and I glimpsed her blond hair and blood on a screw sticking out of the swing set. Aunt Glenna quickly brought an ice pack, and we broke speed limits rushing to the nearest hospital.

Throughout the ordeal at the hospital, from cleaning the wound until the last stitch, I held Kara's hands and kept repeating, "Jesus will help us. Jesus will help us."

What a relief to finally get home. I felt like our day had gone over a waterfall, catching us in the whirlpool beneath, leaving us unable to move on.

Finally, we heard a car in the driveway. Aunt Janice ran out to brief Kara's parents, hoping to lessen the shock of seeing their child with one side of her head shaved and stitched. As they knelt alongside her, Kara sat up suddenly and announced, "Jesus pwayed for me!"

Her mother replied in a choked voice, "Of course, honey. Jesus helped you."

Kara nodded and repeated emphatically, "Jesus pwayed for me!"

And I wondered where she had gotten that idea. I had said Jesus would help us. Had Kara somehow seen or felt Jesus praying for her, standing with her loved ones in the room, making "intercession for us"? Only God knows for sure.

Thank you, dear Lord, that even toddlers can learn that when suffering strikes, you are there. Remind me of Kara's example whenever I face the whirlpools of suffering.

Two Jackets

Take up the whole armor of God,
that you may be able to withstand in the evil day.
Ephesians 6:13

"**G**wandma! Two jackets will be enough!" Kara was adamant, and I was at a loss. It was a damp, cold November day, with a chilly wind blowing. I had decided to take Kara with me to visit my sister Eunice. I knew Kara disliked wearing heavy winter coats, yet I wasn't sure that a sweater and denim jacket would be enough for her to wear on such a cold day. Kara's father pointed out that Kara would be in the car most of the time. Yet Kara discovered that in the short distance to and from the car, the sharp wind bit through the skimpy protective outerwear she had chosen to wear. Two jackets weren't nearly enough to keep out the November chill.

In the book of Ephesians, the apostle Paul reminds us that we need to put on protective spiritual outerwear too. Paul calls this protection, God's armor, listing six articles of protection we need to wear against the darkness and sin of this world. All six pieces complete "the whole armor of God."

Like Kara, we sometimes consider it a bother to worry about protective outerwear. It's easier to leave the coats and hats at home. In the same way we often give little thought to our spiritual outerwear. We don't sense the need for spiritual armor when we are enveloped in the safety of our everyday routines. Kara learned, and so should we, that it is best to always be protected.

Dear Father, thank you for the protection you have provided through your armor. Help me to be careful to wear all of it at all times, not merely settling for two jackets when your whole armor is what's needed to stand against the darkness of this world.

The Old, Old Story

God so loved the world that He gave His only begotten Son, that whoever believes in Him should not perish but have everlasting life.

John 3:16

"Haven't we found it yet?" I ask Kara.

Her crisp instructions are, "Just keep readin'."

Kara has brought me four books of bedtime stories, requesting that I read the titles in all of them because she can't remember the story she wants me to read aloud. Finally, when I am about through the index of the third book, Kara says joyfully, "That's it! That's it! That's the one I want you to read."

Kristin exclaims, "Kara, you've heard that old story a million times!"

But Kara retorts, "I don't care! It's my favrit story!"

I am a lot like Kara—I have a "favrit" story too. And it is an old, old story—almost two thousand years old. I have heard it many times sitting at my mother's knee when I was a small child like Kara. And I have heard it many other times also. It is the story of God's love for humanity, the tale of how he sent his Son to die for our sins.

An old hymn describes my feelings about hearing and telling my "favrit" story:

> I love to tell the story;
> For those who know it best
> Seem hungering and thirsting
> To hear it like the rest.
> I love to tell the story!
> 'Twill be my theme in glory
> To tell the old, old story
> Of Jesus and His love.[3]

Each time I hear this old, old story my spirit is renewed once again by the unspeakable love of my heavenly Father and his Son. Do you have a "favrit" story? I hope you'll find someone to share it with today.

Dear Lord, thank you for the old, old story about your love—a love that never grows old. And thank you for your mercies, which are new every morning.

Thank You for Me

God created man in His own image.
Genesis 1:27

When it was time for bedtime prayers during one of my granddaughters' visits, I noticed Kara said, "Thank you, God, for Mommy and Daddy and Kristin and Kara and Grandma and Aunt Janice. . ." And the list went on.

I had to smile at Kara including herself in the list of people she was thankful for. But then I thought, *Why shouldn't she be thankful for herself? Shouldn't we all be thankful that God has created us and breathed into us the breath of life?*

Kara's simple prayer made me wonder if I had ever thanked the good Lord for myself. I've thanked him for all his bountiful blessings. I've thanked him for being my Savior. I've thanked him for my loved ones, a home, good food, etc. But had I ever thanked him for *me?*

Of everything on the earth or in the deep seas or throughout the high heavens, I believe our own bodies are perhaps the most marvelous of all of God's wonderful creations. The Bible says we are "fearfully and wonderfully made."[4] And within each one of us is a living spirit!

Now, as I daily reflect on the wonder of God's creation, I want to say with the psalmist, "I will sing praises to my God while I have my being."[5] And, like Kara, I also want to remember in the future to thank him for making me, *ME!*

Dear heavenly Father, thank you for creating me. Thank you for giving me a body to use on this earth to enjoy your blessings here, and to house the spirit of life which you breathed into me. I praise your holy name that because of the death of your Son someday my spirit will return unto you.

Searching, Searching

With my whole heart I have sought You.
Psalm 119:10

While Kristin and Kara played in the backyard, Kristin happened to notice her dad carefully locking the outdoor storage shed.

"That's where they are, Kara! That's where they are!" Kristin shouted to her little sister.

"Where what is?" her father asked knowingly.

"The Christmas presents!" Kristin returned triumphantly. "Kara and I searched and searched all over the house for them!"

Their father smiled. He and their mother had gone Christmas shopping early this year, and the children knew it. It had evidently been a wise decision to hide their purchases under lock and key.

Just as Kristin and Kara searched for their Christmas presents, we often seek for things in this world that will make us happy too. Sometimes we feel that if we could just have a new home or a new car or a new job, we would be happy. Maybe we long for designer clothes or perhaps the money to take an extended vacation. We often assume that if we just had plenty of money to buy all the items our hearts desire, our happiness would be complete. However, all too frequently we find that whenever we attain those things we wished for, we only find ourselves longing for something else.

Though our constant search for possessions or positions only brings us frustration, there is one ongoing search that will bring us fulfillment. Only by seeking for the things of God can we find lasting peace and happiness. Jesus, knowing this, said, "Seek first the kingdom of God and His righteousness, and all these things shall be added to you."[6] If we make a wholehearted search for God our first priority, we'll find everything we *need*—and more.

Dear heavenly Father, help me to seek first your kingdom, knowing that you love me and will care for my physical needs.

A Good Picnic

*Peace I leave with you, My peace I give to you; not as
the world gives do I give to you. Let not your heart be
troubled, neither let it be afraid.*

John 14:27

Kara is lonely. She wants to do something special.
"Gwandma," she announces, "let's go on a picnic!"

I am not too enthused, but I agree. We pack sandwiches, drinks, fruit, and cookies, and head off for the park.

Though it is early spring, a hot wind is blowing. I try
to find a table where the hot breezes won't hit us directly,
but the gales seem to be coming from every direction. I give
up and use small rocks to hold the tablecloth down, barely
managing to anchor the drinks and sandwiches so they
won't blow away. But the potato chips do sail off into the
breeze. Kara giggles.

We manage a few more bites and then Kara's half-
eaten sandwich and napkin are snatched away. Kara runs
after the sandwich, but unexpectedly the wind shifts, drop-
ping the sandwich right in front of her. Unable to stop,

Kara's foot slips on the bread and mayonnaise, and in an instant Kara falls, skinning her knee. Kara cries momentarily. I give her my sandwich. And I am relieved when finally the food is gone—most of it blown away, very little eaten. As we climb into the car and start homeward Kara turns to me with a happy smile, stating emphatically, "That was a good picnic."

"I guess so," I respond. But as I reflect I realize it was a good picnic. I spent some time with my granddaughter. And we enjoyed each other's company.

When problems buffet my life as the winds battered that day, the Bible says that we can still go to bed at night and say, "This was a good day!" Jesus promises to give us peace in our storms! And the best way to keep that peace is to spend more time with him.

Dear heavenly Father, when the storms of life come, help me to seek the peace of your presence, knowing that your power will sustain me—no matter what.

I Don't Recognize a Thing!

The Lord had said to Abram: "Get out of your country,
from your family and from your father's house,
to a land that I will show you."

Genesis 12:1

Kara's voice was insistent. "You've gone too far, Gwandma! You're going the wrong way! You've got to turn around and go back!"

"I know, Kara," I told her. "I missed the street, but I think it will save time to turn to my right and try to angle back rather than trying to turn around."

I was supposed to be at Kristin's school by 1:00 p.m. for a special Grandparents' Day program. But first I had to take Kara to the babysitter's home in an unfamiliar area of town. I had made a wrong turn and now I was lost. I turned to my right, hoping to find a through street that would lead me back into the right neighborhood.

Kara wasn't very encouraging. "Gwandma, I just don't recognize a thing! You're clear lost! You are never going to get to Kristin's room now!"

We all have gotten lost at one time or another, wandering on strange streets or in a maze of corridors in unfamiliar office buildings. In the Scripture above, God actually called Abraham to leave his home for an unknown land. Sometimes God's call may lead us into unfamiliar territory— territory where, as Kara says, we "don't recognize a thing." It can be frightening to be where there are no familiar landmarks. But if we follow God's guidance, though we may not recognize all the steps or places along God's path for our lives, we will one day recognize our eternal destination: Heaven!

Dear heavenly Father, help me to be fearless as I tread
the unknown paths you place before me. Help me to say
with the songwriter,
I'll go where you want me to go, dear Lord,
Over mountain, or plain, or sea;
I'll say what you want me to say, dear Lord;
I'll be what you want me to be.[7]

Clearing Our Path

If God is for us, who can be against us?
Romans 8:31

I had gotten lost in an unfamiliar part of town as I attempted to take Kara to her babysitter's home. If I couldn't find the correct way quickly, I would be late for the Grandparents' Day program at Kristin's school. I drove around another corner, and Kara exuberantly exclaimed, "I know where we are! I know where we are!"

Though we had finally reached a street that Kara recognized, right in the middle of the road were two big trucks illegally blocking the road while the drivers talked. Usually I try to be patient—at least for a little while. But that day I was not patient. I leaned on my horn. Beep! Beep! Beep!

Perhaps the determined face of a grandmother behind the wheel influenced the truck drivers. Or perhaps their conversation was finished. Whatever the case, those trucks moved away instantly. Kara giggled. She thought it was funny that the horn on Grandma's little car could make the big, old trucks move out of the way!

Have you ever found an obstacle right in the middle of your path blocking the action you want to take, the direction you want to go? Was there no way around it, over it, or under it? Don't be discouraged! The Bible reminds us that if we are within the will of God, we have a stronger power working for us than whatever is blocking our efforts! Jesus said, "Behold, I give you the authority to trample on serpents and scorpions, and over all the power of the enemy."[8]

Dear heavenly Father, please help me to trust that my hopes and your plans for me can succeed! You promised that with faith I could even move mountains!
Thank you for clearing my path.

Money Is Not Important!

Do not seek what you should eat or what you should drink,
nor have an anxious mind.
...your Father knows that you need these things.

Luke 12:29-30

S ome time ago Kara and I watched a video tape about Davy Crockett. In the video Davy rescues a pioneer family who has mistakenly camped with their covered wagon in the middle of a dry creek bed. Davy persuades them to move because a flash flood is coming. The family leaves reluctantly as the father moans, "But all my money is in that wagon." Just then a wall of water roars down the canyon and the family's belongings float away—including all of the money. Since the family is safe, Davy Crockett and his companion walk off to continue their adventures.

"I wonder what happened to that family with no wagon, or clothes, or money!" I mused aloud to Kara.

"Gwandma," Kara exclaimed, "money is not important!"

I was a little surprised at her vehemence, and I replied soothingly, "No, honey, I guess it isn't." I paused to think and a moment later asked, "What is important, Kara?"

"Gwandma! God and Jesus are important," she explained in a superior tone.

I smiled and told her that she was right. And I remembered the Scripture where Jesus tells us to consider the lilies of the field—to watch how God takes care of them, sending rain and sun, and how he clothes them in brilliant colors. And if God is so concerned about a flower, Jesus adds, won't he be concerned enough to provide for our needs too?

Kara was right. Money isn't important. God is!

Dear Lord, please help me to trust you as the source for my every need. Help me to have faith "as a little child"—unconcerned and confident in your provision.

You Just Can't Trust the Newspapers!

Until your high and fortified walls, in which you trust, come down.

Deuteronomy 28:52

For supper I prepared what appeared to be a delicious vegetable soup taken from a recipe from the "cook's page" of the daily newspaper. The soup smelled appetizing while it was cooking. But something must have gone wrong. The finished product was a disaster.

The adults ate it politely. But Kristin and Kara turned it down cold. I had to break down and make them some sandwiches. Frankly, I wasn't too crazy about the soup myself. "It just looked so good in the newspaper," I remarked.

Kristin spoke up in a warning tone. "Grandma! You just can't trust the newspaper!"

Sad to say, Kristin's observation is sometimes true. Sometimes newspapers contain misprints or incorrect facts. If we place our trust in what we read or see in the media, we are sure to be disappointed.

God's people were warned long ago against placing their trust in worldly things. High, fenced walls might look indestructible, but God's people were cautioned to place their trust in him instead of their walls and gates.

Even though all things in this world change, the Lord does not change. We can trust him to be the same faithful, loving, concerned Father that he has always been because God is "the same yesterday, today, and forever."[9] That makes me want to sing with the psalmist, "O Lord of hosts, blessed is the man who trusts in You."[10]

Dear heavenly Father, please help me to know that there is something solid I can cling to in a world filled with turmoil and fear. Help me to face the future secure in the knowledge that you love me and are always with me.

We Need a Bush Real Bad

*If you then, being evil, know how to give good gifts
to your children, how much more will your Father who is in heaven
give good things to those who ask Him!*

Matthew 7:11

Ihad just purchased two ornamental shrubs at the greenhouse. Kara was with me, and her eyes lit up. "Oh, Grandma! Is one for us?" she asked.

"No honey," I replied, "I didn't know your daddy wanted one!"

Kara quickly retorted, "Oh, Grandma, he would. We need one real bad!"

I hesitated, recalling that their yard already looked pretty full to me. But I couldn't bear to kill the joy in those blue eyes, so said, "We'll buy you a bush, and your daddy will just have to find a place for it."

Kara clapped her hands with joy. "Oh, thank you, Grandma, thank you!" she squealed.

Kara doesn't know how happy it makes me that some of my farmer-heritage blood has shown up in her second-generation veins. But even if Kara did not share my farmer's love for growing things it would make me happy just to be able to provide something for her that she truly enjoys or appreciates. I was as happy to help Kara pick out "her" bush as she was to receive it.

The Bible says that God is like that too. The Father enjoys giving us good gifts even as I enjoyed giving the bush to Kara. Now whenever I pray and tell my heavenly Father I need something, I remember two things: Kara's shining eyes and Jesus' assurance that God is willing to give us good gifts too.

Dear Lord, thank you that I am a joint heir with Jesus. Let this heritage rule my heart, helping me ask for gifts that you will enjoy bestowing upon me.

Please Take Care of You

I have prayed for you, that your faith
should not fail; and when you have returned to Me,
strengthen your brethren.

Luke 22:32

Kristin and Kara's mother and daddy were called to a distant city because of the death of a dear friend. I was glad to care for my granddaughters while their parents were away and to be a help to their family, especially under such sad circumstances. However, it was a rather busy time for me, so I couldn't stay for the entire time that their parents were gone. The "other grandma" agreed to come and help out.

As I packed my things and prepared to leave, Kristin, then in the third grade, handed me a note. On the outside she had written "Read." And when I opened the note I saw the words, "Please take care of you."

Tears stung my eyes. So many times over the years I had been concerned for her and cared for her. Now Kristin had sensed the weariness and stress in my life, and she was concerned for me! As I kissed her goodbye, I told her, "Thank you, Kristin. You can say a prayer for me."

In the Scripture above, Jesus was concerned for Peter—concerned enough to pray for him that his faith would not fail. Without a doubt many times the concern and prayers of my own family and friends have carried me over the rough spots and through the dark valleys of my life. Jesus' command to his disciples that they love one another as he had loved them included the unspoken admonition to pray for each other too. Because of this, I am firmly convinced that until we reach heaven we will never know the full extent of the power of our prayers offered on behalf of others. Is there someone you need to pray for today?

Dear heavenly Father, thank you for the privilege of praying for friends and family during the storms of life. And thank you for the many prayers that have been said for me when I needed them.

More Presents Than We Can Carry

According to your faith let it be to you.
Matthew 9:29

When Kara was five years old, she came down with the chicken pox. Christmas was only a week away, so Kara decided it would make her feel much better if she could open one of her presents from under the Christmas tree each day.

Kara's mother was afraid this wasn't the best idea. "You don't have that many presents under the tree!" she protested. "If you open one each day, you won't have anything left when Christmas gets here!"

Kristin added, "Don't worry, Kara. Just wait until we go down to Grandma's and Aunt Janice's. We'll have more presents than we can carry!"

And true to Kristin's faith and to Kara's utter delight there were lots of presents under the tree at Christmas— more presents than they could carry.

The Bible tells us that if we have faith in our heavenly Father, he will fulfill our requests. Time after time the good Lord has heard and answered my prayers. Why then is my faith not as strong as it should be?

The problem may be that I rely too much on what I see rather than on what I believe. The Lord promises us blessings that are "pressed down, shaken together, and running over."[11] When we focus on his promises instead of on our circumstances we will find abundant blessings, or, as Kristin says, "more presents than we can carry."

Dear Lord: Please help me to walk close enough to thee—
That my prayers will always be,
Something good for others, and right for me.
That thy great power that stilled the wind and sea,
Can be shown in answering my smallest plea.

Seventy-nine Chicken Pox

The very hairs of your head are all numbered.
Luke 12:7

It was obvious that Kara had chicken pox. Blisters were broken out all over her body. And when she left the dinner table to go lie down, I went to sit with her, attempting to comfort her by recalling my experience with chicken pox.

As I reminisced with Kara, I recalled that I had the chicken pox much worse than any of my brothers and sisters did! I told her how my mother decided to count the chicken pox on one side of my face as I lay in bed. I told Kara that I could still remember how important I felt when my mother told everyone I had seventy-nine chicken pox on one side of my face! That was a record none of my brothers or sisters could beat!

Kara responded immediately. "Count mine, Gwandma," she said.

So I counted the chicken pox on one side of her face; there were only forty-two. I told her she wasn't as sick as I had been! That made Kara smile. And even though Kara didn't have as many chicken pox as I had had as a child, it still made her feel important for me to take the time to count the chicken pox she had on just one side of her face.

As Kara drifted off to sleep I thought of how much I loved Kara and cared about how many little spots she had. But God loves us even more than that. Our heavenly Father numbers even the hairs of our heads!

The psalmist said, "How precious also are Your thoughts to me, O God! How great is the sum of them! If I should count them, they would be more in number than the sand."[12] God's love goes beyond my limited imagination, beyond my calculations. God's love goes all the way to eternity.

Dear heavenly Father, how wonderful is your love for me!
Thank you for your great, unfathomable love.

How Many Minutes?

*I waited patiently for the Lord; and He inclined
to me, and heard my cry.*

Psalm 40:1

The phone on my desk rang. It was Kristin again. "When are you going to be home, Grandma?" she asked.

Kristin and Kara were spending some of their Christmas vacation with Aunt Janice and me. Aunt Janice had promised her little nieces that she would take them to school to play basketball as soon as I brought the car home. Now they were waiting impatiently for my arrival. I told Kristin again that I would be home as soon as I could get there, but that it would take just a little while.

Kristin responded promptly, "I know, but...how many minutes?"

I was unable to answer Kristin's question with a specific time, choosing rather to promise to be there just as soon as possible. But her question made me realize that sometimes I am as impatient with my heavenly Father as Kristin was with me. When I call upon him for guidance, I want my answer right now. When I have a need, I sometimes expect God to provide for it on my time schedule.

Maybe some saintly Christians receive immediate replies to their requests, but I don't think I ever have. It seems that God wants me to learn to wait in faith and keep listening. For an answer will come quite often in not too many of God's minutes and usually when I am least expecting it.

Dear Lord, you ordered the days and nights and measured the weeks, months, and years. Help me trust that you will always answer me at just the right time.

What's Aunt Janice Bringing Me?

Receive a hundred fold now in this time. . .and in the age to come, eternal life.

Mark 10:30

Aunt Janice was planning to devote part of her summer to helping a church group overseas. While she and her sister Diana were discussing the trip on the telephone, Aunt Janice heard Kara holler in the background, "What's Aunt Janice bringing back for me?"

Sometimes we can all be like Kara. When some project is being planned we sometimes can't help having selfish thoughts. Whether or not we come right out and ask it or just think the thought to ourselves, we often wonder *What's going to be in it for me?*

The disciples were no different. Peter reminded Jesus that they had forsaken everything to follow him. And then Peter asked, "What shall we have?"[13]

Jesus answered Peter by describing the many blessings Peter could expect to receive. I notice that Jesus included persecutions among the blessings.

Though I have received many blessings in my life, I have never been persecuted for my faith in Christ. Is that a blessing God will yet bestow on me?

In America we have been spared many of the problems that Christians suffer in many lands. Yet I wonder if persecution ever did come to me, would I count it as a blessing? Would you? We must remember Jesus' words that it is a blessing to be persecuted for him. He suffered for us and for our salvation; we should be honored to suffer for him.

Dear Lord, let my faith stand firm on the solid rock.
Please give me strength to rejoice with the
saints through the ages because we are counted
worthy to suffer for your sake.

The Cupcakes

*I say to you, ask, and it will be given to you; seek,
and you will find; knock, and it will be opened to you.*
Luke 11:9

One school year Kara and Kristin's mother accepted a long-term substitute teaching job. The full-time work lasted only ten weeks, but ten weeks can be a long time to children. Five-year-old Kara, especially, really missed having her mommy around every day.

While I was visiting for a couple of days trying to help, Kara came into the kitchen with a problem. The children at preschool whose birthdays fell during the summertime celebrated "pretend" birthdays during the school year. They could take treats to preschool and have a party just like the children whose birthdays fell in the wintertime.

"Grandma, you and me have got to make some cupcakes and take them to school," Kara said, adding, "Mama doesn't have time now."

I chuckled. I loved Kara's confidence in me. She knew I would help her. She didn't even ask. She just said, "You and me have got to do it." She was sure of my love and help, and I assured her that I would be glad to help her have a pretend birthday party.

We need to show that kind of confidence in God and in his love for us. The Scriptures repeatedly illustrate how much our heavenly Father loves his children and wants to help them. And we are reminded that our prayers are not merely a means to convince God that he should help us. Rather, as Philips Brooks said, "Prayer is not conquering God's reluctance; it is taking hold of his willingness."

It may be hard for us to realize that the great God who formed the world, the stars, and the heavens cares about each individual person and wants to help us. But he does, and he will. All we have to do is take "hold of his willingness" through prayer.

Dear Lord, thank you for your tender, loving care, and for your help in all ways, both big and small.

Only Five Days Left

Teach us to number our days, that we may gain a heart of wisdom.

Psalms 90:12

Kara, who usually has a healthy appetite, didn't eat much at supper. Later, as I was brushing her hair before bedtime, Kara turned to me with a trembling chin. "Grandma," she cried, "there's only five days of preschool left! I'm not going to have time for my pretend birthday party now!" Tears welled up in her blue eyes.

"Oh, Kara," I told her, "you have lots of school days left. We have plenty of time to have the party!"

But Kara shook her head. "No, Grandma," she insisted. "Teacher said we just had five days left!"

Both Kristin and I tried to persuade Kara that she must have misunderstood what her teacher had said. Kara's spirits rose a little when we suggested that maybe the teacher meant that they only had five more days until spring vacation. Yet when Kara went to bed she still wasn't sure that we would have time for her birthday party before the school year was over.

Kara was afraid that school time was running out. She wanted to have a birthday party before it was too late. Many times we adults put things off because of a lack of time, money, or energy. Kara's focus on her birthday party made me wonder what we would want to accomplish most if we felt certain that we had only a few days left on earth. The top of all of our lists should be to make sure that we have gained everlasting life by accepting Jesus Christ as our Savior, for there is no worthier goal for any of us.

Dear heavenly Father, someday my time on earth will run out. Help me to make my relationship with you my top priority—accepting you as my Savior and serving you as my Lord.

A Gift for Everyone

Having then gifts differing according to the
grace that is given to us, let us use them.

Romans 12:6

Kara wanted a pretend birthday party with her preschool class more than anything else. So I encouraged Kara to help plan the event. I asked her if she wanted to do something besides serve refreshments.

"Yes," Kara replied quickly. "I want to play that game where there are lots of presents on the table and everyone has numbers."

I knew in a flash what game Kara was referring to. In this game assorted gifts are placed on a table. Every person in the room draws a number out of a hat. Starting with the highest number drawn, each person chooses a present from the table. However, there is one catch. When you choose your gift, anyone with a lower number can confiscate your choice and keep the gift you have selected. Then you have to go back to the table and choose another present.

The game continues until all of the presents have been chosen and/or snatched.

A game in which preschoolers snatch presents from other preschoolers sounded like a risky choice to me, so I tried to persuade Kara that perhaps a different version of the game would be better. But Kara wouldn't budge.

I let the question drop for a moment as I thought about the "game of life." Sometimes we are so busy wishing we could have the same abilities or talents or opportunities as someone else that we never take time to realize and be thankful for our own capabilities.

God gives different talents to each one, and the Scriptures tell us that each person's talent is needed to make the body of Christ complete. No snatching of gifts is needed. What God has given is already the best.

Dear heavenly Father, guard me against the envy of another's gift. Help me to be content to use the talents you have given me in the place where you want me to work so that Christ's body might be complete.

It's My Birthday Party

*You were not redeemed with corruptible things, like silver
or gold. . .but with the precious blood of Christ.*

1 Peter 1:18-19

Kara's birthday party at school was becoming a reality. We compromised on a variation of the holiday gift grabbing game, deciding that it would be better to place numbers on the presents on the table and then have the children draw numbers and match them to the numbers on the gifts. Kara wasn't sure that this variation would be as much fun, but she relented. To Kara's delight, when I picked her up the next day, the teacher and I set a date for Kara's "pretend" birthday party.

On the way home, we stopped by the Christian bookstore to buy little books to use as gifts for the game. As I began to sort through the children's books, I looked for the least expensive ones, knowing that I would have to purchase twenty of them.

Kara protested, "Grandma, it's my birthday party! Let me pick the books!"

I thought, *Yes, sweetie, it's your party, all right, but I'm paying the bill.* Nevertheless I told Kara she could choose the books.

Finally Kara had an assortment of books that pleased her. Her selection included several thin, little books. They were so small I reasoned that they wouldn't be too expensive. Little did I realize that they were the washable kind that cost more than the others did!

Kara's book choicees reminded me that God has given each of us choices in our lives too. At times we choose to follow God. But at times we choose to sin. We may think our sins are trivial or insignificant, but, oh, what an awful cost Christ paid to wash our sins away! Just as the smallest book for Kara's party cost the most money, so our smallest sins cost Christ his life.

Dear Lord, let me never forget to say thank you for the terrible price you paid to wash me whiter than snow.

My Eggs Are Better'n Hers

All have sinned and fall short of the glory of God.
Romans 3:23

Kara and I were coloring Easter eggs. Her mother's instructions had been for Kara to color four eggs and to leave four eggs for Kristin to dye when she came home from school. Both girls were happy with the finished products, and they enjoyed setting up the Easter decorations their daddy had brought them, arranging the pretty eggs in different ways.

When everything looked beautiful, Kara came and whispered softly in my ear, "We won't tell Kristin, but I think my eggs are better'n hers!" I winked at her and smiled. Her secret was safe with me.

Jesus told the story of a man who thought he was "better'n" everyone else, and he didn't mind who knew it! Jesus said that the man even told God when he prayed how good he was. He reminded God that he paid tithes, didn't sin, and fasted twice a week. But Jesus said that God rejected the prayer of the man who thought he was so good, but accepted instead the prayer of a poor publican, who cried, "God, be merciful to me a sinner!"[14]

It is difficult sometimes for people who try very hard to live good, moral lives to realize that they still need a Savior. Of course it is important to live "good" lives, but being good can't save us. If we could have bettered ourselves by ourselves it would not have been necessary for God to send his Son to die for us. But God did, and his Son died so that we could be "better'n" we were and good enough for heaven.

Dear heavenly Father, please help me to realize that no matter how much better than anyone else I may think I am, my own actions can never save me. I still need a Savior. I still need you.

Carrots and Eyes

Their eyes they have closed, lest they should see with their eyes...and turn, so that I should heal them.

Matthew 13:15

Kara was eating the carrot sticks I was trying to fix for lunch about as quickly as I was preparing them. I remarked, "You should have good eyes! Did you know carrots are good for your eyes?"

"Nope," Kara crunched.

Curious now, I asked, "Have you ever had any trouble seeing?" I didn't expect a positive response to my question because Kara had never complained of eye trouble. Yet my own children had had to start wearing glasses for near-sightedness at a very early age.

Kara thought for a moment before she replied. Then she said soberly, "Yes. I do have some trouble seeing."

I stopped my work and stooped to look into her clear blue eyes. "When do you have trouble?" I asked.
Kara replied seriously, "When I'm asleep!" And then she giggled. She had fooled her grandma. And I laughed too.

Jesus spoke about some people in the Bible who had closed their eyes because they didn't want to see. This was no laughing matter. They didn't want to see the truth that Jesus told them because they didn't want to change their selfish, sinful ways. It is hard for all of us at times to follow Jesus' teachings of unselfishness, love, and forgiveness. But the Bible warns that "the wages of sin is death."[15] Only by opening our eyes to God's truth will we find eternal life.

Dear Lord, please help me to open my eyes to your truth and keep my eyes on your path of life so that I might help guide others to your kingdom.

Let's Take a Walk

He took them and went aside privately into a deserted place.
Luke 9:10

Kara was watching a little wistfully as some of the older children played baseball. I asked her if she wanted to go for a walk with me, but she shook her head. Though Kara was too little to join in the fun, she couldn't bear to leave the scene of the action. To my surprise, Kristin suddenly threw down her bat and left home plate. "Grandma, I want to go with you!" she called as she came running to join me.

I was a little astonished—and thrilled! This busy little third-grader is involved in so many activities: homework, piano lessons, choir practice, and sports, which she loves so dearly. Her basketball games overlap soccer practice; soccer games overlap softball practice. Softball games merge with swimming all summer long, until it's time to start the whole schedule all over again!

Because of her busyness I sometimes have felt crowded out of Kristin's life. But now she takes my hand, and I want to catch the moment and hold it forever in my heart. We walk slowly and talk, and I feel the closeness we once shared when she was smaller.

Sometimes my own schedule is full to the brim, and I wonder later *How long has it been since I just pushed everything aside and took a walk with Jesus? Has he been crowded to the outer extremities of my days?*

How about you? Is your schedule too full for the Savior? Wouldn't today be a good day to set everything aside and take a slow walk with Jesus?

Dear Lord, forgive me if my values get twisted. I know you are the most important person in my life. Would you walk and talk with me for a while just now?

Does God Holler?

Hear my cry, O God; attend to my prayer.
Psalm 61:1

Kara is upset. "Grandma! You didn't holler me down!"

I have just told Kara that I am afraid there isn't enough time to get her dressed and get her hair combed the special way she wanted for preschool today. She had been upstairs in the family room, watching cartoons. Though I explain that I had called her three times to come downstairs, Kara objects again, "But Grandma! You just didn't holler me down!"

Sometimes I am like Kara. I wish God would "holler me down"—especially when I am doing the wrong thing. After all, even traffic cops raise their voices or blow their whistles to halt us in our tracks if we break the law!

But does God holler? He has a mighty voice, of that I am sure. One time when he spoke from heaven to his Son, the people said his voice sounded like thunder.

But God has never hollered at me. In fact, I have to listen very carefully for his still small voice.

There have been a few times in my life when I have heard what I believe were very quiet but audible words from God. Yet often when I seek his guidance, I wonder if he's heard me at all. When my heart finally grows still, then I sense his presence and his quiet answer comes. Though he may not holler at me, God still manages to get my attention and answer my prayers. And that's really what matters anyway.

Dear heavenly Father, forgive me for feeling discouraged at times, for I know that if I am patient you will hear and answer my pleas. Thank you for guiding my way even if you never "holler me down."

An Everyday Grandma

The Lord is my shepherd; I shall not want.

Psalm 23:1

I have mentioned to my daughter my concern that some of the "specialness" of being "Grandma" diminishes when I care for the children for too long a time. My daughter's words give me a choice when she replies, "It all depends, Mom, on whether you want to be an 'everyday' Grandma, or just a 'good-times' Grandma!"

Smiling, I respond quickly to those choices. "I want to be both!" I proclaim.

I love the girls' companionship. They are most certainly my pride and joy. Yet reality proves that I am sometimes cross and gruff. I know that my strength doesn't seem to hold out as long as their needs do. And I don't want our precious love to be marred by the nitty-gritty annoyances of the daily grind of life.

Although I want to be the kind of person who can be their special friend—their "good times" Grandma—I am reminded that God is my "everyday" companion.

He rejoices in my happiness, and keeps track of my tears. He is always there when I need him, ever loving and kind. So maybe what my granddaughters really need is an "everyday" Grandma—someone who is dependable, loving, caring, and always there with enough energy left to give a hug or to speak an encouraging word.

Dear Lord, thank you for being my everyday companion all of the time, whether in the valleys or on the mountaintops.

I'll Help You, Daddy

I have made the earth, and created man on it.
I—My hands—stretched out the heavens, and all
their host I have commanded.

Isaiah 45:12

I call across the kitchen, "Kara, please set the table for Grandma. Your mother will be home soon, and we'll eat."

Kara and I have been out for a long walk, and I am hurrying to fix the evening meal. But Kara's little legs are tired from the walk and she declares, "I'm tired, Grandma."

I remind her that I am tired too, but then I ask, "Don't you want to have supper ready for Mommy?" Kara replies with a yawn, "Yes. I want to have supper ready. But my legs are still tired."

As we continue to debate the issue, her daddy comes home. Then Kara has an idea. "Daddy," she says, "if you will set the table, I will help you!"

Kara's daddy could have set the table all by himself in less than five minutes if he had wanted to. He really didn't need Kara's help, but together they set the table anyway.

I fear that I have often approached my heavenly Father in the same manner. I know at times I have prayed, "Oh, God, if you will just do such and such a thing, I will help you do it! I will give you my tithes and offerings. I will give you my service."

But does the God who created the heavens and the earth really need my help? I don't think so. Yet I do know that God has heard those "I'll help you" prayers. And when those prayers were offered in accordance with his will, there have been times when we have done the job together. God may not have needed my help, but I'm sure glad he let me pitch in.

Dear heavenly Father, thank you for hearing my prayers—even though at times they are presumptuous. Thank you for graciously allowing me to work for your kingdom.

Decisions, Decisions

*You will guide me with Your counsel, and afterward
receive me to glory.*

Psalms 73:24

My preoccupied mind isn't paying much attention to the little passenger I am driving home from preschool. But when I hear her words, "I been figgerin' and figgerin' 'bout two things," I think to myself, *You and me, too, sweetie-pie.*

Aloud I ask, "What two things, Kara?"

"I been tryin' to figger out," she responds, "whether to stay a whole week with you and Aunt Janice, and I been tryin' to figger out whether to play T-ball this summer!"

I suppress a smile. Kara's preschool finished a week before Kristin's school, so I had asked her if she wanted to come visit me all by herself. I didn't realize that my invitation would become such a big problem. I begin to chuckle, but suddenly stop as I realize that the problems I have been trying to solve are surely as small to God as Kara's problems are to me. Yet God never laughs at my concerns. He takes the time to hear and answer them.

After a moment I tell Kara, "If you come down to spend the week with me and you get homesick, I will drive you home." And I add, "I think you would like T-ball, but if you didn't, you could always quit!"

The sunshine breaks through on Kara's sober, little face. Someone has shared her problems and cares about her decisions. My heart is lighter, too, as I remember that someone cares about my decisions and will give me the guidance I need to make good ones.

Dear heavenly Father, thank you for hearing my problems and giving me guidance. Thank you for taking the time to listen to my smallest difficulty.

Assistant Coaches

He said to them, "Go into all the world and preach the gospel to every creature."

Mark 16:15

Kara's voice was indignant. "But Daddy, what am I going to be?"

Her daddy, as the coach of her older sister's soccer team, had originally told Kara that she could be his assistant coach. She had even blown the whistle for him when he told her she could. But now she felt her daddy had betrayed her because he had enlisted the services of another assistant coach.

Noting the storm clouds on Kara's horizon, her daddy soothed her ruffled pride by pointing out that the new helper was only going to be the "goalie" assistant coach. Her father wisely mentioned that a soccer field was a big place, adding that he might even have to have another assistant coach or two. But Kara was mollified when she was assured that she would remain the head assistant coach.

The Bible says that Jesus' disciples complained to him one day that someone else was preaching in Jesus' name and even performing miracles! The disciples were upset and jealous, fearful for their position as Jesus' spokesmen. But Jesus said that they should leave the other person alone because "he who is not against us is on our side."[16]

Jesus recognized the need for assistant coaches. When he prepared to return to heaven, he gave his disciples a tremendous responsibility to share the good news of salvation with everyone. He knew that there would have to be lots of assistant coaches in the game of evangelism to do the job right—for the world is a mighty big field!

Dear Lord, I know the fields of the world are ready for the harvest of souls. Help me to work with my other assistant coaches for your glory—even though they might not be doing it exactly as I think they should!

You Can't Say That!

To whom little is forgiven, the same loves little.
Luke 7:47

After much thought and contemplation, Kristin, then nine years old, had decided to acknowledge her faith in Christ as her Savior and be baptized. Shortly thereafter in the midst of a childish spat, Kara yelled, "I hate you!"

Kristin replied promptly, "I hate you too!"

But Kara quickly responded, "You can't say that! You've been baptized!"

Isn't that how life is? The world looks at the church and says, "Those people claim to be Christians, but look how they act!" Or one Christian judges another by saying, "How can he say he's a Christian and do that!"

All too often we forget that none of us are perfect. We all fall short of keeping God's laws no matter how hard we might try. But when Jesus died on the cross he took upon himself the burdens of our imperfections. He bore the load of our guilt and shame. Jesus paid for our sins and granted us forgiveness. As a result, we should be eager to forgive others.

To illustrate this point Jesus told the parable of a man who was forgiven a large debt by his superior. Though released from his debt the man, in turn, would not forgive his neighbor a small debt. Jesus said that by his refusal to forgive, the man ultimately lost his own forgiveness!

Sometimes we judge each other in white-hot anger over some minor offense. Feuds can develop from small disagreements and last for years! As Christians we should not act this way. How can we harbor hateful feelings against someone else when we have come under Christ's forgiveness?

Dear Lord, thank you for bearing my penalty for sin. Help me to remember that since I have been forgiven much I must also forgive much.

When Are You Coming?

Men of Galilee, why do you stand gazing up into heaven?
This same Jesus, who was taken up from you into heaven, will so
come in like manner as you saw Him go into heaven.

Acts 1:11

"Grandma," Kara's small voice asked on the telephone, "When are you coming?"

I replied, "I'm getting ready to load the car now. I will be there pretty soon. When did you want me to come?"

Her reply was emphatic. "I want you to be here right now."

Kara's impatience reminded me of how anxious my mother always was for Jesus' return. She was so fond of the Scripture in the book of Acts where the angel told the disciples that Jesus would return one day. Down through the ages Christians have longed for Jesus' return, expecting him to appear any day. On each letter my mother sent to me she would inscribe, "Jesus is coming soon," or "Jesus may come today!" But still Jesus tarries. And still Christians wait.

Though I am frightfully cognizant of my imperfections and shortcomings, I know that my Savior died to pay for those sins. I am fully persuaded that my future is in heaven. But why am I not as hopeful as my mother was for Jesus' return?

Facing facts honestly, I think it is because I have friends and loved ones who do not share my faith. They still need to know Christ as their Savior. I want passionately for them to have the same relationship with him that I have. Perhaps that's why Christ tarries, for the Lord is "not willing that any should perish."[17]

Dear Lord, I know that we all will have to spend eternity somewhere. Let me live my life in such a way that others might be persuaded to trust in you and make heaven their home.

You Just Play 'Em!

My yoke is easy and My burden is light.
Matthew 11:30

Kara believes that grandmas are supposed to know how to do everything. So she can't quite believe that I can't play the piano. She had asked me to play a song for her on the piano, and I had admitted that I couldn't read sheet music.

Kara is amazed. "It's easy, Grandma! I'll show you how," are Kara's words. Taking the sheet of music and pointing to the notes she tells me, "See these little black things here? These little things tell you which keys to play—and, well, you just play 'em!"

With some effort I convince Kara that there is a little more involved in playing the piano. Nevertheless she is quite disappointed in my inability to play the song she wanted to hear.

Though there are skills in this life that are difficult to master (like playing the piano), serving the Lord doesn't have to be one of them. Sometimes people hesitate to surrender their lives to Christ because they fear he will require them to do something that will be impossible—or at least very hard. However, Jesus tells us that his yoke is easy and his burden is light. He promises to give us rest for our souls.

God knows each one of our talents and abilities—after all, he gave them to us! And he would never require us to do anything that we are incapable of doing.

God also promises to give us the Holy Spirit to help us in any service we undertake for him. If we truly believe this, we cannot fail in any task the Lord gives us to do—even if it means learning to play the piano!

Dear heavenly Father, help me to remember that whatever you ask me to do doesn't have to be done alone. I have you to help me—and that is a restful thought.

I Only Fell Down Once

*Our light affliction, which is but for a moment, is working
for us a far more exceeding and eternal weight of glory.*

2 Corinthians 4:17

Kristin had long tried to persuade her mother to let her ride her bicycle to her piano lesson. Though the distance was only eight blocks or so, there was one very busy street to cross. Finally, Kristin's mother relented, and Kristin was thrilled to venture out alone!

Kristin made it to her lesson on time, but she came into her teacher's music studio with both knees dripping blood. Yet Kristin wasn't distressed. She cheerfully announced, "I only fell down once!"

The teacher, who was a good friend of the family, furnished Kristin with some first aid spray and bandages, and they got on with the music lesson. Kristin was so happy to have been able to make the trip alone she didn't even seem to mind her seriously skinned knees.

The apostle Paul suggests that as we travel our Christian journey we should overlook any injuries we suffer along the road just as Kristin ignored the skinned knees she received on her first solo bicycle trip. So what if we get a few bumps and bruises as we travel? Our Savior, who loved us enough to die for us, has promised that he is going to prepare a place for those who love him, and what a wonderful place that will be. If we can keep our sights set on our eternal destination and the glories of eternity, we won't worry about the hurts that come our way in this life. Instead, we'll apply the first aid spray of God's faithfulness and the bandage of his love to our skinned knees and bruised feelings and keep pedaling along on our journey of faith.

Dear Lord, thank you that the joy of my final destination will far outweigh any problems I encounter along the way.

Look What These Cost!

Shepherd the church of God which He purchased
with His own blood.

Acts 20:28

Kara took my hand as I entered the door. She pulled me over to the couch and showed me two new pairs of shorts—one pair for her and one for Kristin.

"Grandma," she exclaimed, "just look what these cost! Grandma Helen brought them to us!"

The girls' other grandma, Grandma Helen, quite often purchases small items for the grandchildren while shopping. Because there usually is no special occasion for these gifts, Grandma Helen often brings them by without removing price tags. I was a little startled at the price. There wasn't a yard of material in both pairs! The little shorts were cute, but what a price to pay for them!

As I thought about today's high prices, my mind wandered to the highest price ever paid for anything in the world—the price Christ paid to free us from our sins. The Bible says he "loved us and washed us from our sins in His own blood."[18] Christ could have paid no greater price for us. He paid for us with his life.

But there is another cost factor involved in the story of salvation—the cost of rejecting Christ as Savior. What good will all the expensive things in this world do us when death claims our body if we have rejected God's final call of grace? The words from an old hymn put it this way:

If you reject God's final call of grace,
You'll have no chance your footsteps to retrace—
O hear his call, O hear his call![19]

Dear Lord, you paid a terrifically high price that I might have eternal life. Thank you, Lord, for dying for me!

We're Not Brothers!

He, wanting to justify himself, said to Jesus,
"And who is my neighbor?"

Luke 10:29

Kristin and Kara were spending the weekend with their Aunt Janice and me. They wanted to play a card game before bedtime. Though it was late and they were both a little tired and cross, we agreed to play a quick game. During the game, mischievous Kristin teasingly tried to pull a card from the middle of the draw pile, rather than taking the one on top.

"You can't do that, stupid!" Kara exclaimed.

"Oh, Kara," Aunt Janice protested quickly, "you shouldn't call anyone stupid! Did you know it says in the Bible that whoever calls his brother a fool is in danger of hell fire?" (Matthew 5:22).

For one split second, lattle Kara's face registered great concern. Then, in relief, she cried, "But we're not brothers! We're sisters!" It appeared to Kara that because of a technicality the verse in Matthew was in no way applicable to her!

Kara's rationalization parallels a lawyer's who long ago asked Jesus, "And who is my neighbor?" In the parable of the Good Samaritan, Jesus made it quite plain that the neighbor we are commanded to love is anyone in need. There are no excuses or loopholes in God's law. We must love and be kind to all people, helping whenever necessary. In God's eyes, all people are "brothers" and "neighbors" regardless of skin color, status in life, occupation, or any other difference between us.

Dear Lord, please help us by your grace and power to love and minister to each other without seeking an excuse to eliminate anyone from your mercy.

Lots of Character

The testing of your faith produces patience.
James 1:3

Kristin wanted me to come to one of her basketball games. She was in the fifth grade now and playing on a girls' team in a league. Aunt Janice and I agreed to come to a Saturday morning game and rose early that day to make the fifty-mile drive and to arrive on time. Both teams played their hearts out. It was exciting. In the last few minutes of the game Kristin's team was ahead by one point. Yet in the last two seconds the opposing team scored a lucky shot and won the game.

Aunt Janice and I accompanied a disappointed Kristin and the rest of the family to a restaurant for a late breakfast. Aunt Janice, seeking to console Kristin, counseled, "Anyone can win and be a good sport. But when you can lose and still be a good sport, that builds character!"

Without missing a beat, Kristin mumbled dejectedly, "Well, I should have lots of character! I've lost enough basketball game!"

Kristin thought she had all the character she wanted. Sometimes we share that feeling. We aren't quite sure that we want to be more patient or be better Christians. Yet the book of James counsels us to rejoice when problems beset us. We're reminded that persevering through trouble will make us stronger in our faith. We can learn and benefit from each trial that comes into our lives.

Dear heavenly Father, thank you for your never-failing help when circumstances seem overwhelming. Help me to remember that you have always worked things out for me.

I Read the Last Chapter

*God will wipe away every tear from their eyes; there shall
be no more death, nor sorrow, nor crying. There shall be no more
pain, for the former things have passed away.*

Revelation 21:4

Kristin explodes into the kitchen exclaiming, "I read the last chapter! I already know they have to leave because they are in Indian territory."

"But Kristin," I sigh. "That will ruin the story for you!"

"No, Grandma! I still like it," she replies. "And I'll read all the rest too!"

I had given Kristin a set of Laura Ingalls Wilder's books for Christmas, trying to encourage her to share my love for the printed word. Yet now, after asking her how she likes the first volume, I feel slightly perturbed that she has read the ending before finishing the rest of the book. But, I muse, if she learns to love to read, I guess it really doesn't matter if she reads the end before the middle or even before the beginning.

As I turn to other chores, God gently reminds me that I have read the last chapter too—the last chapter, that is, of the greatest book of all. I've read the last chapter of the Bible, but that hasn't suppressed my desire to read the rest. I know there is much between the first and last chapters of the Bible that I still need to explore.

I pause and thank our heavenly Father that he has given us this last chapter, for it is full of assurances that the promises in God's Word will be fulfilled. Though my way grows weary and sorrows come, these assurances of God's fulfilled promises sustain my steps on the journey of life.

So, I smile as I reflect on Kristin's reading habits. Reading the last chapter might not be so bad after all.

Dear God, thank you for the last chapter.
Thank you for picturing the better land waiting for
me in your kingdom.

And We'll Talk

*Even the youths shall faint and be weary—But those who
wait on the Lord shall renew their strength.*

Isaiah 40:30-31

"**K**ara, won't you please come with me on my paper
route? Come with me and we'll talk!"

Kristin's voice has a pleading note. Now fourteen
years old, Kristin shares a paper route with her little sister,
Kara, who is now ten. Kara receives a smaller share of the
profits for delivering the "inside," shorter route, while
Kristin's route is much longer.

Tonight, however, Kara's route is finished while
Kristin hasn't even started her route. Kristin just arrived
home from basketball practice. Her legs are already tired,
and the route looks too long and dreary to walk it alone.
Kara agrees to go, and I smile—not only because I know
Kristin wants the company, but I expect she is also counting
on a little help!

How wonderful it is to find someone who is willing to
walk with us on our journey of life and lend a helping hand,

a shoulder to cry on, or an ear to bend. Those dear ones truly understand Paul's admonition to help carry "one another's burdens, and so fulfill the law of Christ."[20]

But sometimes those willing helpers are already busy. During those times when I think I'll have to go it alone, when my work ahead looks tedious and long, I find that my load is made much lighter when I ask Jesus to go with me. He has promised that I'll never have to walk alone. And he's good company because he helps too!

*Thank you, Lord, that you are always willing to walk with me
and talk to me and help lighten my load
when I am weary.*

Are You Going Home Today?

In My Father's house are many mansions; if it were not so,
I would have told you. I go to prepare a place for you.

John 14:2

Pssst—pssst. I hear a hissing noise and groggily turn my head on the pillow

Pssst— There it is again. And then a whispered, "Are you going home today?"

My eyes flutter open. It is early in the morning, and the rest of the family is sleeping. I had been, too, until Kara's little figure appeared by my bed asking, "Are you going home today?"

Kara knows that I was planning to go home today, but this event is becoming a ritual. Whenever it is time for my visit to end she asks the same wistful question, "Are you going home today?"

Now I tell her, yes. I am going home. But I promise to write her a letter. And I also promise her that I will visit again soon.

Pushing aside the weariness that I feel, I rise to keep her company until the rest of the family awakens. I recognize that my weariness is harder to throw off than it used to be. The weariness makes me realize that I am not as young as I once was. And the weariness reminds me that someday I will be going home to my eternal home.

Hopefully, when that time comes, Kara and Kristin will be grown and quite possibly teaching little ones of their own about Jesus and the eternal home that they can have with him. And as they look forward to the time that they will go home to their eternal home, they will know that Grandma is waiting for them there.

Dear Lord, thank you for the heavenly home you have prepared for me. I look forward to seeing you and old friends there too.

Acknowledgments

[1] Taken from "Somebody Cares" by Fannie Edna Stafford. Copyright © 1910, Renewal © 1938 by The Rodeheaver Co., Owner. *Hymns for Praise and Service,* circa 1958.

[2] Taken from "They'll Know We Are Christians by Our Love" by Peter Scholtes. *Hymns for the Family of God.* F.E.L Publications, Los Angeles, CA: 1966.

[3] Taken from "I Love to Tell the Story" by Katherine Hankey. *Hymns for Praise and Service,* circa 1958.

[4] Psalm 139:14

[5] Psalm 146:2

[6] Matthew 6:33

[7] Taken from "I'll Go Where You Want Me to Go" by Mary Brown. *Hymns for Praise and Service,* circa 1958.

[8] Luke 10:19

[9] Hebrews 13:8

[10] Psalm 84:12

[11] Luke 6:38

[12] Psalm 139:17–18

[13] Matthew 19:27

[14] Luke 18:13

[15] Romans 6:23

[16] Mark 9:40

[17] 2 Peter 3:9

[18] Revelation 1:5

[19] Taken from "God's Final Call" by John W. Peterson. Copyright © 1961 by Singspiration, Inc. *Great Gospel Songs and Hymns.* Published by Stamps-Baxter Music of the Zondervan Corporation, Dallas, TX: 1976.

[20] Galatians 6:2